Cataracts

Carlos Harleaux

Copyright ©2020 by Carlos Harleaux.

All rights reserved. This book or any portion thereof may not be reproduced or used in any manner whatsoever without express written permission of the publisher except for the use of brief quotations in a book review.

First printing, 2020.

ISBN – 13: 978-0-578-78052-8

Book Cover Design and Photography by Chris Booth

Interior Design and Typesetting by Stewart A. Williams

Printed by IngramSpark in the United States of America.

7th Sign Publishing
P.O. Box 300
Missouri City, TX 77489

IT WAS ALL A BLUR

I know what you're thinking. 10 years later and I still don't have this thing called life figured out. You would be exactly right to make that assumption. My first book, *Blurred Vision*, was released in 2011 and detailed specific poems about having a blurred state of mind. Today, I'm wiser than I've ever been but also more uncertain than ever. True, there are some aspects of life I now view with 20/20 vision.

However, there are other parts of life where my vision is cloudier than ever before. The last 10 years have been a blur to say the least. Honestly, my greatest lesson has been to learn to enjoy the ride…. and try not to repeat the same mistakes along the way.

2020 alone was a sting that none of us could have predicted. This book is a collection of the thoughts, lessons, and ideas I've collected along the way. Ultimately, I am not the same person I was 10 years ago. I've grown and evolved into a better version of myself. Still, there's a lot of work to do.

CONTENTS

It Was All a Blur* iv
Love Life 1
Margaritas 2
Caption This 3
Ghostbuster 4
Turn Me On 5
Elated 6
Need You / Want You 7
Let Love Breathe 8
DND 9
America's Hidden Treasure 10
Keep Your Honesty 11
Play Me Hard 12
Own It 13
Punching Bag 14
Journey to the Lighthouse 15
Curve 16
Blink^ 17
Foresight^ 17
Cracked Screen^ 17
Tears^ 17
Shoulda 18
Woulda 19
Coulda 20
Best Kept Secrets 21
Matchbox 22
Check Out Time 23
Cold Sheets 24
Before You Leave* 25
Fast Forward 26
Uno Out (for Love) 27
Walls 28
Inhale You Again 29
Happy 30
Could You Call Me? 31

Black Is Not a Trend	32
Love vs Hate	33
Road Trip	34
A Moment of Clarity*	35
Until	36
Soot	37
Rings and Things	38
If You Love Me	39
Your Favorite	40
Low Battery*	41
Stream Your Love	43
Not Guilty. Not Innocent	44
Know Better	45
More Than You Deserve	46
New Heart, Who Dis?	47
Somebody's Gonna Love You	48
Justify My Love	49
Distance, Space, and Time	50
Meh	51
Plagiarism	52
Unwrap Your Angst	53
The Right Words at the Right Time*	54
A Different Lens	55
Spare Me	56
Resistance	57
Slaying Dragons	58
Melatonin	59
Four-Out-of-Seven*	60
Ooh Honey^	61
Sour^	61
Bitter^	61
Scorched^	61
The Sixth That Slipped Away	62
Cataracts	63
Blinding	64
Love Life	65
ABOUT THE AUTHOR	66

denotes an essay

^ *denotes a haiku poem*

LOVE LIFE

Love has a way of making a fool out of us
All those things we said we'd never do
End up being the very thing
That keeps us bonded to
Reflections of love that
Don't amount to its full glow
We justify intolerable acts of selfishness
Masked as love and make excuses
Just to have the broken pieces
Of a masterpiece we so desperately try to salvage
For our ego's sake
We knew it would all fall down
Before all the bricks were laid
Our debts are paid
Yet we carry the baggage
Into every situationship and relation
If we let it all go
Maybe then our love would
Have space and time to grow

MARGARITAS

The sweet grit from the salted rim can't apply
A salve for the damaged soul within
So I take another sip
On the 22nd of loneliness
Guess the separation only goes to show
Top shots only prolonged
The numbness from the top shelf sting
Little did I know the burn was so near
And the chill so fierce
The clock strikes 11:00 and then 12:00
As the lights flicker
A passive signal for me
To find my way out of here
It's closing time soon
Sip sip, drip drip
Now I'm spilling my emotions all over my shirt
Everyone is so busy enthralled in the throws
Of this national holiday
They think I'm a perfectly designated
Puzzle piece to the celebration
Oblivious to my contemplative stance
While they barely hold up the wall
Little do they know it's a literal catch 22
But they'll never understand
So I just raise my empty goblet and
Tell the bartender to
Refill it for another one
Or maybe two

CAPTION THIS

If we captured a still frame
Of this very moment
What would our eyes witness?
Scantily clad intentions from
Emotions we can't keep contained
Would our umbrellas even matter in the streets
Where justice seldom reigns?
We are trained to view the lens
Without fully comprehending the disastrous
Work of art that lies before our
Eyes have not seen the shudder
From the reflection of our individual souls
Double edged words
Cannot be retracted
Somewhere along the way our
Priorities came reeling off tracks
Adapting to the pop life
Subbing lies for truth that weren't even worth
The original snap
Is the state of our existence
Even worth captioning?
I'll wait and stay close
To the state of the union
Of my own ties that scream to be unbound
Ease my own mind that yearns to be unwound
The problem all along was I kept focusing on
The story of how everyone else's
Staged uploads came to be
I forgot to focus on the relevant issues of us and me
Imagine that
Caption this
Undressed naked eyes can see
Beneath filters, hashtags, and memes

GHOSTBUSTER

Extinguish my flame
And poof...before my flesh cools
Your soles hit the floor
I'll leave the latch off the door
For your inevitable return
That's what she said
No text back
Your cologne lingering in the wind
The reasons that we're here
Have me in my feelings
When you're far and when you're near
I won't answer next time you call
That's what she said
I could restrict my desires and
Neglect my own pleasures
The ones I know you like
Turn on all the lights
To avoid seeing you slip into the darkness
But that is where you like to keep me
That's what she said
Who you gonna call if it ain't me?
That's what he said
Ghostbuster

TURN ME ON

You always get your juices flowing
Long after dusk has settled
As the branches dance across the window
Capturing me like a thief in the night
I like it like that and
I won't put up a fight
But I'll still let you tie me up and
Wait for the hairs to rise
On the back of my neck
Such a euphoric release
While you whisper in my ear
All good things must come to an end
But let's make this one linger
Longer than the last drip drop
Of moisture we can muster
Must you continue to do this to me?
Who am I kidding?
I wouldn't have you any other way
Keep turning me on

ELATED

My inner glow no longer matches
The illuminating light on my phone
When your text arrives
That excitement has dimmed
Perhaps I should be elated
To see your name
Flash across my screen when you call
But I am quite complacent in the way
Things have come to be and
Wish for nothing greater
The desire for more has left
With the midnight train that rolled
Out of here several moons ago
I guess I should love or like your posts
At the very least
But I simply won't devote the energy
To provide you with any artificial satisfaction
I'll keep scrolling instead
That moment has fizzled out
Like the disappointment of the first sip
Of a soda that has lost its carbonation
Maybe I should consider myself privileged
To be the recipient of such attention
That only transpires when your options have run dry
I tried to muster up that same thrill and flame
That once lived here but now
There's nothing left but an empty, cold room

NEED YOU / WANT YOU

Don't tell me you need me
Needs fulfill obligations that
Eventually foster into resentment
Tell me you want me
Wants develop into desires that
Grow into insatiable bonds and
Catapult us into another galaxy

LET LOVE BREATHE

You say I let you go
That I was so nonchalant
Brushed you off like I didn't care
Dismissed you like our time didn't matter
That is the furthest thing from the truth
I think deep down you know it too
I've just grown weary of fighting
Don't have the mental capacity to argue
So I'll let you be right this time
Whatever you say is probably true
It's unfair to negate your feelings
If that's what you choose to believe
If that's what helps you sleep at night
We've both exhausted enough energy
We've both given blood, sweat, and tears
Not to mention all the years
But love sometimes ain't enough
I'm not letting you go
I'm just letting love breathe
Be free

DND

My surroundings are still
Sheets of ice
Miles high and wide
I am but a droplet of water
Wishing to disturb the monotony
Wishing to throw a wrench in
All the calamity I see
But the world is set to
Do not disturb
It can't hear me
Clawing
Exclaiming
Protesting
For something meaningful
Something brighter
Something grander than
This perpetual state of being
No need to ring the alarm
They won't hear it anyway
I've got to find a way to
Make my disruption heard
Will you join me?

They will never understand how it feels
To experience the grimacing stares
When I enter a room
Their body language acts
In direct opposition to my presence
My creativity is theirs for the taking
Without proper credit due
They use my strength to mask their weakness
Oblivious to the apprehension I face
Each time I walk outside my door
I look over my shoulder not knowing
If this will be my last time
Seeing my sons and daughters alive
Or will an unprovoked altercation
Be the event of my demise
I am expected to remain silent
While my dignity
Is hitched to the back of pickup trucks
Tucked heads with a poker face of steel
Aren't ideal but predictable in this
State of the world
I am a threat to society
Let them tell the story
I am the most under-represented
Undervalued and overlooked being
That walks this earth
Though I helped give life to so much of it
The black woman

KEEP YOUR HONESTY

You can keep your truth
I don't need your proof
Unless it comes bottled up with
At least 40 percent
Here it is straight, no chaser
Whether little white ones or
Ones that swallow us in black holes
They're all still the same
Funny how that works
Who's right? Who's wrong?
I don't really care
Just don't give me a reason to
Question your integrity
Don't give me a glimpse beyond the
Curtain to your inauthenticity if you have any
If you must and if you wish
I can handle your honesty
But honestly, keep it to yourself
And your guilty conscience too
If you're really untrue then
I'm afraid it's truthfully all on you

PLAY ME HARD

It's your turn to make a move and
You're holding on to your poker face
Tighter than the vice grip you have on me
I just can't figure you out
What are your true intentions?
If you're playing me then
I'd rather you keep it on the low and
Wrestle with your own conscience in the dark
So unlike me to lack
A spirit of discernment
If you're playing me
Don't straddle the fence
Push it to the limit
Put the pedal to the medal and
Drive me crazy why don't you
If you're playing me
Don't play me easy
Give it all you've got

OWN IT

As I mentioned at the beginning of the book, the last 10 years have been quite a blur. One of the biggest lessons I've learned during that time is how to own my happiness. Honestly, I prefer to use the word joy because happiness is momentary and depends on the situation. Whether it's a romantic relationship, familial relationship, or friendship, we must remember that we are in charge of our own mental well-being. People are human and imperfect beings. As a result, one of the few constants with people is that they will always disappoint us.

I believe many marriages fall apart because one or both parties put the fate of their happiness in someone else's hands. Not only is that an extremely unfair burden to put on someone, it's also unrealistic. What makes us happy on Tuesday may change by Thursday. What made us happy in 2015 may not suffice in 2021. Things change and so do people... all the time.

I found that when I started owning my happiness, regardless of the actions of others, I was...well, much happier. Don't get me wrong. I'm a work in progress, just like all of us. However, the moment I let everyone else off the hook for supplying my happiness, I find it in that same instant.

PUNCHING BAG

Scratched, bruised, battered,
But not broken
I was built for this
I was made to absorb your
Doubts, fears, indiscretions, and
Even sweep your most idiosyncratic proclivities
Under the rug
I snap back into place
Just as you left me on your last hit
I may squeak a little at the hinges
But I am front and center…
Dedicated to the cause
On your mark, set, go!
Braced for the next blow
But every now and then
The punches make me a little delirious
Every now and then, the upper cuts
Make me lose my equilibrium
I was built for this
I was made to absorb your
Frustrations, insecurities, shortcomings and
Even ignore some of your angriest moments
That I took the brunt of
For the sake of making you stronger
But honestly, punching bags gets tired too

JOURNEY TO THE LIGHTHOUSE

You lead me back to the shore
Tranquil and peaceful
Amidst the turbulent waves
I somehow feel fearless
My back against the crest
And my feet touching the trough
Of the ocean bed
This is mental clarity
and telepathy all in one breath… underwater
Can you feel it?
The tide is turning, I greet it
With a welcoming smile and
Buoyant spirit
This is oneness in a sea of
Infinite calamity
Float on
Stream on
Swim on
To your lighthouse
May your journey
There be well worth each stroke

CURVE

Like that scent everybody wore
In high school
We thought we were the cool kids
To smell like the grown men and women
We raced to be
Until we get here and realize
It's not all It's cracked up to be
We thought that scent would draw them closer
And now as adults we concoct all
The right pheromones
Show interest in all the things we
Don't really give a shit about
We laugh at jokes that fail to land
Flying high
On the wings of a fantasy
That hasn't materialized
When I look in your eyes I wonder
If you know how it feels to dodge
All the feels from those that were real
Only to authentically be curved by you
Go figure

BLINK

Just like that it's over
Before I lift my eyelids
Take a blink. Rinse. Repeat.

FORESIGHT

I wish I knew now
Bumped my head again instead
Won't be a next time

CRACKED SCREEN

Touted you safely
Handled with care and still fell
Oops, we are broken

TEARS

You thought I would cry
I'd rather let the sweat sting
You won't get that

SHOULDA

Maybe I shoulda cheated
Now I understand the plight of Keysha
We could never reach a resolution
Too busy filling our empty spaces
With false allegations and accusations
Love is only complicated when its
Actions are misappropriated
You incubated your own insecurities
Now watch them hatch
I shoulda left the latch on my heart
Instead I left the gate open for mass destruction

WOULDA

Maybe if I whispered sweeter nothings
In your ear that would have kept you satisfied
It was all a dream and seemed like
Our relationship status changed overnight
Literally I figured we would reconcile
Reunite under one domicile
What we woulda done is
water under a bridge that has crumbled
To a point of no return
The same flame that sparked us
Is the same one that made us burn

COULDA

Maybe if I rewound the clock
Our time spent coulda been more picturesque
Yet instead the brush strokes are beautifully chaotic
Our love song is melodically and sonically inept of
Finding the right groove
It's too late to cry over spilled wine
So why try to decipher the right decision
When I've already made my bed
Frankly, the mattress is more comfortable here
I loved harder than I intended
Perhaps deeper than I ever imagined....oh well

BEST KEPT SECRETS

They stir like a brewing pot
Boiling at the pit of our stomachs
Rolling in the deep with toils at
The thought of someone like you
They haunt us in the middle of the night
Shake us awake and
Break us into a panicked sweat
Ain't nothing sweet about 'em
Smile in our faces and laugh
Behind our backs
Footsteps in the dark
With invisible tracks
But we know where they've been
We recognize their whispers
We do as they command of us and
Keep them under lock and key
To what avail
Are our souls ever released from the jail
We've enclosed them in?
They scratch beneath our skin
As they grow weary of being confined
Show me yours and
I promise to show you mine

MATCHBOX

Pass me that box so I can
Strike one, strike two
Save yourself now if your
Antiquated ideals you want to hold on to
The smoke is billowing
Suffocating your stubborn ways
Light it up
Watch the flickers dance
Upon the curtains
Up the walls and through the roof
Save yourself now if your
Unfounded principles you want to cling to
Strike three strike four
Too hot to touch the doors
Now you're stuck inside
Of what used to be the funhouse of your own mind
Trapped as the flames envelope your subconscious
Exploding your expectations into unrecognizable pieces
That remain when the ashes settle
Now wouldn't that be beautiful?
Anybody got a match?

CHECK OUT TIME

I hope you've enjoyed your stay
Seaside waves underneath starry nights
Crisp white linens and room service
Being catered to you every need and
Some things you didn't
Yet and still I felt you deserved it
A toast to a fairy tale we both
Knew wouldn't have a happy ending
I was always too stubborn and
You were always too slick for my liking
Oh the clock strike 10 past 11:00
I'll help you get your things together
I'll never forget the memories we made
It was fun for an extended stay
A few blissful nights
But now it's check out time

COLD SHEETS

The coolness of the sheets
Grazing my skin
Is typically a euphoric sensation
Right before I drift off to sleep
But tonight, nothing will warm their presence
If the present is a gift
Maybe I should return to sender
Because this feels like a burning entrapment
Yet, I still feel cold
It's all your fault
You should be here to thaw this chilled heart
Somehow, I knew from the start
This would be our ending
Yet the truth stings sharpest in the
Thickness of the moment
In the belly of love's beast
Only you can save me from
Its snarls and snares
I can see my breath before my eyes
Before I eventually fall asleep
With you absent in the physical
Only close inside my mind

BEFORE YOU LEAVE

Have you ever noticed that before you break up a relationship, end a friendship, start a new job, etc., that the person or thing you're leaving suddenly gets their act together? Of course, there are two sides to a story and no one is perfect. However, I've found that often times right before I make the decision to move in a new direction, change finally comes. In the past, I have allowed this to make me stay in situations longer than their expiration date.

As I've gotten older, I've learned that goodbyes don't have to be ugly. Goodbyes don't have to be filled with expletives and ill feelings. Goodbye just simply means that person or situation no longer suits your life at that very moment. Maybe fate will bring you back together again. If it's meant to be, it will be. Nonetheless, there's value in knowing when your time is up, in any situation.

I believe that leaving a situation at an appropriate time minimizes heartache, confusion, and resentment for both parties. Once our emotions change, it's easy to stay in unhealthy situations because they may "feel right" at the moment. In the long run, it usually culminates in nothing good. Am I saying throw in the towel at the first sign of adversity? Not at all. But we must have the discernment to see past the facade of feelings and act on our reality.

FAST FORWARD

As the years began to pass
So swiftly like a freight train to
Our respective destinations
I sometimes wonder what could have been
If we remained on the same route
And pressed fast forward
Held on a little longer
Suffered through the grit to
Smolder the clouds of confusion
That loomed as stagnant dark clouds
Above our heads
We couldn't stand the rain
This much is true
You're doing well
We're both just fine and
Stronger for the journey but
At times I can't help but wonder
Where we'd be now
Like those triumphant episodes of
Behind the Music when the band
Weathers the storm long enough
To witness the sunlight dance upon
Their faces
Would love have still danced
Upon our hearts now
Or would we be right back here?

UNO OUT (FOR LOVE)

Draw Two
One heart split down the middle
Trying to pick up the pieces
I never meant to break it
The color is red on the left
Wait the right half switched the color blue
The number was 4
Though the first 3 were much closer
Skip you and your feelings
You skip me back and
Pull out your wild card
Draw Four
Unlucky relationships to follow
With a reverse to seemingly bring the luck
Back in your favor
Now the color is green
With envy for the nonchalant attitude
You so effortlessly displayed
This game is never ending
We have completed the entire deck and
Added another until we arrive at
This very moment
Two cards in each hand
Another yellow reverse to symbolize
Your bending of my perception to see
Things your way
Now we both proceed with caution
I drop my last two cards to
End the rigamarole
Two Draw Fours for you
One yellow and one red left in my hand
I'm so blue
Uno out on this game called love
Sometimes a win is more than we
Came to the table to lose

WALLS

I too, have built them high
So I recognize yours
Though softer, wetter, and less rigid
They are still the same
Still untamed and unable to
Crumble at the touch
If I could just get inside them
Surrounded by their epicenter
Too tall to climb over and
Too dense to tackle
I wait patiently to explore them
I curiously imagine the texture, smell, and decor
Of the beautifully complicated sanctuary within
I plead anxiously to implore their
Crumbling invitation to
Get in the middle of your.....
Walls
One day you will let me in to
View their radiant splendor
From the inside out
For now, I'll dream of dew settling
On their unforeseen glory

INHALE YOU AGAIN

Spring rain and ocean breeze
Can't compare to the lingering scent of you
I am immediately catapulted back to
When my senses were heightened
Pushed to their limit in such an exhilarating fashion
I have yet to find a time so divine
It may be toxic but I enjoy
The excitement your essence brings
Now I'm having to inhale deeper to
Relive the intoxicating fragrance of your perfume
It's been too long and your presence
Is slowly dissipating
Come back before it all fades

HAPPY

Plastic smiles with
Tangible expendables
Spine shivering sex....ooh
A moment of silence
Faith, family, and freedom
Or the relentless pursuit
To cross a finish line that doesn't exist
The audacity to think we can
Tame such a moving target
Existential circumstances
Avoiding our own sobering silence
Expecting others to pin down
Our fleeting desires and
Make some sense of the
Blurred mess we made
Happiness doesn't preempt joy
Until we uncover the difference
Between those two fraternal twins
We'll always be unhappy

COULD YOU CALL ME?

Could you call me today?
I know you're busy with
The weight of the world
Placed strategically on your shoulders
As not to let it fall and
Shatter to the ground
But I so desperately need you....
Your voice, at least
Since I am not able to experience
All that your aura is in person
It soothes me
It moves me
It comforts me like a warm, quilted blanket
In the dead of winter
Gives me flowers to ponder for days to come
And bloom in spring
I need you
If only for a minute
That would last me a day or two
A fix to settle my feening desires
Quench me, cool me, drench me
In your wet, silky sweet tone
This may be a request so far fetched
That your eyes may never see the letter
My mouth speaks to write the words
That linger in the air as they travel cross towns
And bump the beds of those sleeping way over....
Well, you know the rest
I need you
I need you to call me
Could you? ... Would you....please?

BLACK IS NOT A TREND

We are more than melanin hued skin
Full lipped pouts and bouts of
Frustrated contortion
Clear the distortion and
See what lies beneath the surface
Of your elementary understanding
We never yearned for your inclusion
Because we built the very tables
You exclude us from
If our existence was so vile
Then why try to emulate
The voluptuous curves, sun-kissed complexions
Broad shoulders, and kinky hair
That dignify our culture's existence
Give credit where credit is due
Being black is more than a
#BlackLivesMatter hashtag or
Bass thumping, soul-infused rhythm
To add a swaggered hitch to your get along
Being black is standing up when it's uncomfortable
Like our ancestors who boldly
Triumphed over insurmountable obstacles
Before social media was a glimmer
In the internet's eye
Why do you still treat our existence
As the latest trendy fad?
We are here to stay beyond
Whether our existence is in vogue with your agenda
Or if it rips it all to shreds

LOVE VS HATE

Love forgives:
It baptizes us where the water
Is crisp, cool, inviting, and
Easier to ingest
Than the perilous tides of
Hate that swallow us whole

ROAD TRIP

Objects in the mirror
Are closer than they appear, along the journey
Though a few mile markers may have pained me
I'd still take the same course
Because it makes the trip
That much more interesting
Although the passengers may rotate
I'm still on course and
Where I'm supposed to be
Some detours, whether self-inflicted or
Imposed upon me were not wasted
Despite what onlookers may perceive
I was built for this
Red light, green light
Some lessons were learned the hard way
Because I failed to proceed with caution
But hindsight is 20/20
And it gave me more precision
In my vision
For the uphill travels to come
Turn up the music and pass the snacks
Let's see what the next rest stop brings

A MOMENT OF CLARITY

"It's good to see you, Director." These are the words I would hear from my Pastor, Sylvester Duckens, Jr., PhD., every time I returned home to Houston, from Dallas. He made it a point to always tell me that when he saw me. I never questioned what made him want to address me as a director. Honestly, I didn't care. I liked it; I felt honored that someone of his intellectual and theological stature would even address me as such.

Pastor Duckens had a way of making people feel special, myself included. Many teachings from his sermons rang true in my life over the years as I grew from a boy into a man. Pastor Duckens made his transition in July of 2020. Although the COVID-19 pandemic prevented me from attending his funeral, I think he knew how I felt about him. That gave me a sense of comfort.

He was never a man who complained, even in his last days. Sometimes I could tell he wasn't feeling his best but he would always say, "Oh, I'm doing alright." There are people in life, outside of your parents, who help shape your thoughts and values. He was definitely one of those men. So much so that I initially had a difficult time finding a church in Dallas when I moved there to attend college in 2003. Again, because of who he was and how he was, it was a challenge to find a church in Dallas; one that really felt like home.

Now, I still carry his guidance and words of wisdom. In a world of unclear vision, he was a bright spot of clarity. I'm grateful to have known him and proud to have called him my pastor.

UNTIL

I forgot all about you
Not a care against the wind
Ignored your texts
Conversed nonchalantly
But when our lips locked
I inhaled you and
I knew I wasn't done

SOOT

Our love once burned
With a fiery glow and
Fragrant oil that slicked our souls
It was magical
Beyond anything my practical
Mind could fathom
Though we dimmed at times
We always found a way to
Add more fuel to the fire
Within us
It burns at the thought now
It's flaky and itches at the touch now
All that remains
Has combusted
Disgusted with ourselves and
How we let it be
Charred soot to ashes
Love in burning misery

RINGS AND THINGS

The perceptive glitz and glamor of
2 equals 3, 4, and 5
Doesn't impress me much
It doesn't motivate me for inclusion as such
Sure, it looks pleasing to the eye
And feels sensational to touch
But I'd rather keep commemorative t-shirt instead
I prefer my cups and my heart to remain
Exactly where I left it last
The concept of commitment isn't what
Makes me timid
It's all the pots calling kettles black
That want you to join in on the fun
I have still yet to see
For some it may fit like a glove
For some it may soothe their psyche and
Rock them sound asleep
I prefer my piece of peace
Over rings and things
No disrespect to whichever you prefer
But as for me, I'm where I wanna be

IF YOU LOVE ME

What's the hesitation?
Who put the pebble at the bottom
Of your shoe and made you
Walk with such trepidation?
I thought our love was gravy
Then again, you prefer the
Non smothered crispness of your freedom
So I take two steps back
With my hands still latched
Allowing you room to breathe
But if love conquers all
Shouldn't it cancel all your doubts
Eliminate your fears and place your better
Judgment aside to intertwine your heart with mine?
Oh me, oh my
I can't fathom you trying to decide
Whether or not I'm worth it
Whether or not we bear the hurt and
Keep trudging forward
If you love me
Then that should be enough, right?

YOUR FAVORITE

I made your favorite tonight
Complete with all the trimmings
Add a heavy hand of love as I
Whisked the finishing touches
A few extra shallots and a clove of garlic
Peppers for an extra zing
Just enough to make the beads of sweat
Glisten across your forehead
Although I detest the taste
I even added a few mushrooms
In your honor and slid them on the
Edge of the plate
Let it rest at a slow simmer
Unlike the raging boil of our anger
This will be my last time
Making your favorite
Since you won't be here to eat it anyway
After tonight, only my taste buds matter

LOW BATTERY

Setbacks are always my greatest source of creativity. Of course, I don't wish for negative things to happen in life just to bring creative juices. However, I've learned to recognize the reasons behind some of my biggest creative moments in life. Year 2020 was no different. Many of us started off this year claiming our time of "perfect vision" and realizing our dreams.

As 2020 has nearly ended, I've realized that this sentiment is still true for me. In many ways, the Covid-19 pandemic was the slowdown I so desperately needed. I was getting burnt out of my daily routine (although I did not realize it at the time). I am a natural introvert, so quarantine didn't bother me much in the beginning. However, the stress of work pressure, depressing news headlines, and a couple of personal issues eventually made it hard for me to relax.

I remember right around the time after the 4th of July, I tried listening to sounds of water before going to sleep on a weeknight. It was a stressful day and that was the only thing that calmed my mind. Later, I noticed that pattern continue as I couldn't relax my mind at night without the crashing waves of water. That was a sign that my battery was getting low, but I didn't notice it at the time.

As the stress of not being able to separate work from home, among other things, started to pile on, I realized this was my chance to pivot. Pivoting in a new direction is never comfortable in the beginning. I like to compare it to breaking in a pair of new shoes. The more you put one foot in front of the other, the process helped me find new ways to get reconnected with my creativity and recharge. This very book you are reading today was not even supposed to happen. My original thought was a re-release of the original *Blurred Vision* book in 2021, with a new cover and a few new poems. Instead, I used that idea to commemorate the 7th anniversary of *Hindsight 20/20* and work on an entirely new project to commemorate the 10th year anniversary of my first book.

Has the journey been difficult at times? Yes. Has every moment been worth it? Most definitely. I believe everything happens for a reason and if we pay attention, every moment brings us closer to our purpose. Are you charged up enough to take advantage of your next opportunity?

STREAM YOUR LOVE

I didn't step into this
Fully immersive experience
Just to get pennies on the dollar
I want the new scent of
Peeling off your layers and
Opening you up inside
As you let me read the
Deluxe edition liner notes
And eventually unlock
The vault you never let the others into
I want to hold it in my hands
Embrace every note and
Ride the syncopated rhythms
Even when they begin to stutter
I want you to take me back
To your deepest fears and regrets
Let them hiss as they awaken
Like the precise needle on hot wax
I want the backstage pass as
I give you the VIP treatment
Your love is too good for
Pennies on the dollar
I want more and
I'm willing to pay for it

NOT GUILTY, NOT INNOCENT

Things will never be the same
Now that we've all seen the light
We were so used to walking underneath
The dimly lit streetlights
Hung out way past dark
With not a care to the wind
Until the sunrise exposed us and
All of our imperfections back then
We fell blindly in love and other things
Headfirst into uncharted territory
We celebrated our unions and
Broke a few along the way
Welcomed new lives and wondered about the ones
That never came to be
Toasted to the victories and
Got toasted even harder to numb the pain
No longer naive but unsure if
We ever truly wanted it that way
We just reveled in the simplicity of it all
Due to no fault of our own
We didn't realize the sun would rise
To shine and provide a sober, blinding light of truth
We weren't ready for it
But we must trudge forward with what we know
We must put our childish ways aside
Now that we know better or better yet, worse
Than we did before

KNOW BETTER

You always did know
Better when hindsight
Struck half past 20:20
Clairvoyance, a looking glass
Into territories we already crossed
Navigating all the tides and troughs
You knew better
Little did I know I smoldered
My own better judgment too
Just to please you
I guess I knew better as well
Yet I didn't vocalize it and
My mind is tired as hell
With my body soon to follow
You know better and I'll let you
Covet that victorious title
I just want to know
Since you knew so much
Can you tell me how we ever ended up here?
In all your infinite wisdom and knowledge
Couldn't you have put out the fire before
The first flame flickered?

MORE THAN YOU DESERVE

This is no ordinary love
Funny how we grow into
The things we don't understand in the moment
We fail to latch on to
What captures our inner peace
So busy living for the moment
I offered and you declined
By your actions
Until that random wyd text
Unread to this day
You still have yet to see the dismay
This is no ordinary love
But you're playing ordinary games
Expecting extraordinary gain
Your expectations are warped and
Disproportionate to your minimal efforts
I'm not up for an ordinary love or
Giving you anything more than you deserve
No pain no gain can
Wait for another day

NEW HEART, WHO DIS?

Teflon chambers
Titanium valves
Molten lava runs through my veins
Where the blood used to flow
They say let it go
Yet I still keep holding on
Harming myself, becoming
An igneous rock
Than can't be penetrated
Calcium buildups make it impossible to
Break inside
A thirst for hydration remains
Though the desire to pursue it subsides
I don't try to say goodbye, I do
Without choking
With a poker face so stiff
You wouldn't recognize
New heart, who dis?
Love don't live here anymore

SOMEBODY'S GONNA LOVE YOU

It's a jagged pill to swallow
A little bit ironic
And a beaten path to follow
An uphill climb that burns
Just as fiercely coming down
I could have loved harder
I could have pushed further
Pride, I could have tucked it away
Trust, I should have placed more in you
Regrets
No
But would I change the past?
Yes
I know you will rise from
The ashes of us with new wings
Fly boldly in the direction
Towards the kind of love you need
Somebody's gonna love you better
Too bad it's not gonna be me

JUSTIFY MY LOVE

Ready, set, go
Tell me in 140 characters or less
How I'm the best you've ever had
Better yet I'll double my generosity instead
Fill my empty ego
With your hollow promises
Like a cardboard box full of
Packing peanuts
My desperation is permeating through
The bubble wrapped insta-snapped stories
Protecting their existence from the outside elements and
Bludgeoning opinions
I like when we play the type of kissing games
That today's millennials could only dream of
Double tap that and let's show
How our relationship goals came to be
I need you to justify my love to you
Through your public validation of we
For the mass majority of people who will
Casually scroll past our captured moments

DISTANCE, SPACE, AND TIME

Distance, space, and time
Leave a crack in the door
Just wide enough for clarity to creep in
Only if we are open to heal
Healing, pain, and forgiveness
Are the seemingly unholy trinity
Pushing us past comfortability
When our hearts are too weak to convict
Conviction, introspection, and trepidation
Cause us to proceed with caution
Because we remember what it feels
Like to have our feet to the fire
That fire drives us to propel ahead to
Better days, brighter nights
Unleashing the chains
But some would rather
Be confined to that fire
Feel all the burns and
Bump their head instead
Distance, space, and time
Should have changed my heart by now
So why does it still beat for you?

MEH

Wanderlust gone bust with nowhere to be
Void of periwinkles and eye twinkles
This love has yet to reach
A boiling point or
Freezing temperature
It just....is
We just.....are

PLAGIARISM

Are your feelings really your own?
Or did you just take mine and
Twist them for your own benefit
I'm climbing and believing in the latter
Time will tell if what you feel is real
Or if you're just lip syncing to a song
You don't even know the words to
Girl, you know it's true
Don't plagiarize my love

UNWRAP YOUR ANGST

I take on your anxiety
Filling the empty space betwixt us
Flooding every orifice until
It consumes your entire existence
Your mind yearns for a comfortable place of rest
But you've exhausted your last dose of melatonin
And everyone else around you is
Five miles to empty too
Can I remove your coat of doubt and
Throw it on the floor?
Leave your weary shoes of weeping
Soiled with broken promises
Right behind the door
Let me be your refuge
Precisely collecting all your fears and timidness
Like throwing darts in the bullseye
I sigh in silence
We all need a moment
Remove your gloves too
So we can experience the essence
Of your unique touch
The universe needs it as do I
Undress all of the garments that
Weigh you down
Untie the blindfold blurring the vision
Of your mind's eye
Unwrap your angst
Before it poisons your existence

THE RIGHT WORDS AT THE RIGHT TIME

I'm a firm believer in everything happens for a reason. However, I also believe we can do or speak certain things to steer our lives in a certain direction. The words we speak and even our thoughts have a great impact on the outcome of our lives.

Positive thoughts and affirmations are so important. We are flooded with so many reasons why we shouldn't be successful, at peace, or just something as simple as keeping a smile on our face. This year marked one of the first times I witnessed words I spoke in anger come to fruition. I remember speaking on the phone to a friend about how I gave myself a specific date for a situation to change. Honestly, I was being a bit irrational despite my serious tone.

Within the next couple of weeks, my life literally unfolded toward what I said was going to happen. Although I spoke the words out of anger, it was truly how I felt. As a result, my life's scenarios were starting to play out just as I said they would. Be careful of the words you speak and when you do, speak the life you want to see.

A DIFFERENT LENS

The lens with which I see you
Was speckled with good intentions
Mixed with doubts, fears, and lies
All I saw were the bright spots of
A twisted fantasy that never was
Caked with residue from the rain
All those times I wasn't wise enough
To cover up
Yet I still saw the beauty
Underneath the layers of flaws
Until I switched my vantage point
Changed my focus and
The lens is much clearer now
Transparent to your beauty or lack thereof
Honestly, I don't like what I see

SPARE ME

I'm putting it all in your court
Or at least 80%
But I'd rather you not settle
If I'm just that 20% that holds
Your attention for the moment
Don't feel like I can't take it
Don't tip toe around what
You perceive my ears
Prefer to receive
I can take the sting
Even if it burns
No animosity
Just another lesson learned
Transparency may just leave me
Vulnerable and easy for the taking
Advantage of; that is
You have the upper hand
But I can't tell how you want to play it
You must be trumped back
Cause only hearts are leading in this hand
Understanding plays a large account
For overcoming old baggage and prior doubts
Seeing messages pop up on your phone
Wondering if you're playing me
Am I not the only one
Unbeknownst to me, your senses may
Tell you the same
I just ask if it's a game
Just let me know early enough to
Take one for the team
And forfeit these feelings
No matter how desperately I wanna be the MVP
I'm asking you to spare me
If it ain't real

RESISTANCE

My actions may tell you no
But you know better
Yes, I need & want you here
Feels smooth like butter with you
All I ask is you don't make me a fool
Don't make me live with regrets
Only your presence filled with
All the love this heart can get
Walls crumbling down
I'm afraid for you to see
Straight through me
Something tells me
You already see me
Just don't take it for granted
Make me pull more into myself
Than I'm willing to give to you
Resistance is high
But my grip is loosening
Can I let go with you?
Can I give in to this tug of war?
Truth is, my guard is already wavering
All I ask is you don't make me a fool
Damn this resistance

SLAYING DRAGONS

Hearing your voice today
Made me reminisce a bit
Back when I felt those flutter flies
Just from seeing your name on paper
That bubbly feeling like dropping skittles
At the bottom of a Sprite to catch that
Sensational taste you have to be there to feel.
From this side of the grass what I felt for you was real
I imagine yours is greener
Time has lessened the necessity for pointing fingers
But do you remember those butterflies
Fluttering through to the dial tone?
Late nights falling asleep on the phone
Kisses of honey
Oh honey, do you recall those times?
I do, now we don't
The butterflies have migrated
To a more comfortable climate
Now the dragons have come out of the shadows
To extinguish the fire that once burned brightly
Our love became a casualty to their breathing wrath

MELATONIN

Let me ease your mind
When the world seems
Too heavy to bear
Give me your fears and
All the things that bound
Your heart in turmoil and
Make your blood boil
Lay them on my shoulders
For safe keeping
Let your thoughts sink
Into my pillow
Let me offer you
A sip of me to unwind
Give your feet a rest from
Walking through the forest
Of your purpose
Let me listen to understand
Void of judgment
Be your diary to keep
All your secrets and
Just be….free
Let me be your melatonin
Float away and
Rock you sound asleep

FOUR-OUT-OF-SEVEN

If 2020 taught me nothing else, it reminded me that life is short. Really short. Of course, this is something we all know but it really hit home for so many facets this year. From COVID-19 to Black Lives Matter and even fallen celebrities that seemed to have gone too soon. I feel like this year has been difficult enough as it is to not allow any unnecessary stress.

Stress really is a silent killer. I've always kept a four-out-of-seven principle that helps me manage stress….as best as I can. Are there things I still have difficulty managing? Oh yeah. But trust me, this rule helps. If any person, place, or thing gives you grief or stress for four days out of a given seven-day week, get rid of it. We are all imperfect people and I've learned not to set high expectations for people that will ultimately let you down.

However, if something is repeatedly causing you pain, most of your time (four-out-of-seven days in a week), leave it alone! We all have bad weeks, even bad months sometimes. Even with that said, nothing is worth weighing you down. Once a person or situation has you bound four-out-of-seven days in a week, the majority of your energy just exited your body and landed on that person or thing. Is that the kind of life you really want to live?

OOH HONEY

Intoxicated
Enveloped inside of you
I don't want to leave

SOUR

A new taste creeps in
My lips pucker as do yours
This love is changing

BITTER

I am not upset
My teeth are grinding tightly
I am highly pissed

SCORCHED

You should have told me
Never knew it would consume
The scabs heal slowly

THE SIXTH THAT SLIPPED AWAY

No sweet tarts or candy hearts
Sappy drips of residue from
All the words we wished to speak
Yet couldn't because our hearts are so full
On the sixth, we don't exist
As a unit, clad in iron armor
I imagine your heart has a similar cage
Surrounding it too
No amethyst glow
Which would have been so apropos for us
A sea of purple, white, and turquoise cala lilies
Crushed beneath our feet
As we travel in separate directions
I feel like such a ninny at times
This oak tree has been uprooted and split
Down the middle
There's no riddle or clever way to say
It was over before it began

CATARACTS

They told me not to chase you
But I kept on anyway
Until I plunged in your waters
Unaware of the depth and turbulent tides
I tried to swim with the current
But you made it impossible for me to see
Any amicable existence between you and me
This cloudy love has obstructed my vision
Empty promises left unfulfilled
The smoky mirrors made my reflection unrecognizable
Waterfalls wash away the residue
Of all my better judgment
Somebody lead me to the lighthouse
To signal for help because I'm in too deep
My sanity is no longer yours to keep
Our love was a blur that remains
Emblazoned on my mind's eye
Although neither one of us wants
To be the first to....well, wait you did utter it first
Guess it's time to say goodbye

BLINDING

I'm peering through the blinds to find your love
Since you've kept it hidden from me in broad daylight
Cracked traces of the sun might shed truth
On the dark past and unpredictable future
We have found our feet firmly mounted in
Love is not blind
But we like to put blinders on to block the truth
Covering up the screams of sound justification
We have placed on mute
I open the blinds a little wider to find your love
But to no avail
The illuminating glow from the outside world
Is just a false pretense of a promise
That was never meant to be kept
In order for me to keep my sanity
I must close the blinds
On the notion of ever finding your love
And open them for my own freedom

LOVE LIFE

Consumed with the consumption of
Perceptions that love brings
Meanwhile another life is taken on the street
Guess it gives us controversial commentary to tweet
Upset because you curved me for curving you
We mismatched our priorities of
What love should really be
Too busy holding up our walls
While the world around us comes crumbling down
We do it for the goals, likes, and approval
Of those who cry in the dark
Perplexed about the state of the world and
The condition of our mental state
Meanwhile love has let us down
Slipping through our fingers
Yet we decide to stay
External love is not the end all
Or litmus test of your worth
Love of self is what matters most
Before you can love anyone else
It starts from within first

ABOUT THE AUTHOR

Carlos Harleaux is a poet, author, blogger, speaker, and publisher (7th Sign Publishing). He is originally from Houston, TX, and currently resides in Dallas, TX. He enjoys expressing art through poetry and fictional writing, as therapy for himself and others. *Cataracts* comes full circle, 10 years after his debut poetry book, *Blurred Vision*.

His other works include a novella entitled *A Swipe in the Wrong Direction* (2020), which is a spinoff of the novel series that includes *Fortune Cookie* (2015), *No Cream in the Middle* (2017), and *When the Cookie Crumbles* (2019). He also co-authored a novel called *Only for One Night* (2019), with Akela Renae. His other poetry compilations include, *Hindsight 20/20* (2013, 2020 [the 7th anniversary edition]), *Honesty Box* (2014), *Stingrays* (2017), *Commissioned to Love* (2018), and *Eleven: Things We Never Said* (2019).

Visit peauxeticexpressions.com to view the entire 7th Sign Publishing book catalog. Follow Carlos's blogs, and receive updates on future projects.

www.ingramcontent.com/pod-product-compliance
Lightning Source LLC
Chambersburg PA
CBHW071413290426
44108CB00014B/1810